Writing Persuasively

Getting Your Ideas Across in Business

Kathleen A. Begley, Ed.D.

A Crisp Fifty-Minute™ Series Book

This Fifty-Minute™ book is designed to be "read with a pencil." It is an excellent workbook for self-study as well as classroom learning. All material is copyright-protected and cannot be duplicated without permission from the publisher. *Therefore, be sure to order a copy for every training participant by contacting:*

THOMSON

COURSE TECHNOLOGY

1-800-442-7477 • 25 Thomson Place, Boston MA • www.courseilt.com

Writing Persuasively

Getting Your Ideas Across in Business

Kathleen A. Begley, Ed.D.

CREDITS:

Product Manager: **Debbie Woodbury**
Editor: **Ann Gosch**
Production Editor: **Genevieve McDermott**
Manufacturing: **Denise Powers**
Production Artist: **Nicole Phillips, Rich Lehl, and Betty Hopkins**
Cartoonist: **Ralph Mapson**

Trademarks
Crisp Fifty-Minute Series is a trademark of Course Technology. Some of the product names and company names used in this book have been used for identification purposes only, and may be trademarks or registered trademarks of their respective manufacturers and sellers.

Disclaimer
Course Technology reserves the right to revise this publication and make changes from time to time in its content without notice.

ISBN 1418864811
Library of Congress Catalog Card Number 2002103322
Printed in Canada by Webcom Limited

2 3 4 5 PM 06 05

Learning Objectives For:

WRITING PERSUASIVELY

The objectives for *Writing Persuasively* are listed below. They have been developed to guide the user to the core issues covered in this book.

THE OBJECTIVES OF THIS BOOK ARE TO HELP THE USER:

1) Learn the importance of persuasive writing skills in most business communications

2) Understand how the S.A.L.E.S. model can help writers sell intangible ideas

3) Explore sensory styles and how to appeal to readers' senses

4) Discover how classic sales techniques can be adapted to the writing process

5) Review writing terms and techniques for conveying information in the most direct way

ASSESSING PROGRESS

Course Technology has developed a Crisp Series **assessment** that covers the fundamental information presented in this book. A 25-item, multiple-choice and true/false questionnaire allows the reader to evaluate his or her comprehension of the subject matter. To download the assessment and answer key, go to www.courseilt.com and search on the book title or via the assessment format, or call 1-800-442-7477.

Assessments should not be used in any employee selection process.

About the Author

Dr. Kathleen A. Begley, owner of Write Company Plus in West Chester, Pennsylvania, loves words. And she knows how to put them together to get people to do what she wants.

Before becoming a professional speaker, Kathleen worked full-time as a writer for several prestigious publications, including the *Philadelphia Inquirer,* the *Chicago Sun-Times,* and the *Seattle Times.* She has authored several books as well as a long list of video-tapes, training materials, and e-learning tools. She publishes a monthly electronic newsletter, *Write Tips,* available at www.writecompanyplus.com.

Listed in several editions of *Who's Who,* Kathleen holds a doctorate in business education from Wilmington College in Delaware. Included in her academic program was yearlong research on the best methods of teaching writing and business communication. She earned her bachelor's degree in English from Temple University and her master's in political science from Villanova University.

Kathleen has absolutely no sales resistance and, thus, tremendous respect for the persuasive abilities of silver-tongued salespeople. Among those who have inspired absolute awe in her through the course of her life: the Chevrolet salesman who talked her into a car before she had a driver's license; the Moroccan merchant who got her to spend $75 for a 75¢ Coca-Cola; and the Moto Photo clerk who sold her $500 worth of holiday portraits of her two Portuguese water dogs.

Her e-mail address is KBegley@writecompanyplus.com. If you're a salesperson and use the writing techniques in this book, Kathleen may well buy what you're selling.

Preface

To succeed in the business world, the ability to write well has always been a given. But to really take your success to the next level and give your writing an edge, it's essential to know how to win over your readers and persuade them to buy your ideas.

This book converts classic sales principles into writing strategies. The concepts apply in documents as diverse as e-mails about breaches in the no-smoking policy, letters recommending a friend for a job, and proposals seeking approval for a four-day workweek.

The underlying message of this book is that all business writers are also salespeople. And, as such, you ought to use some of the tried-and-true techniques not just of sales writing but of face-to-face sales. Sales writing, remember, is defined as writing that gets people to buy your products and services. *Writing persuasively* is writing that gets people to buy your ideas.

In *Professionalism in the Office*, author Marilyn Manning gives an excellent rationale for writing that sells: money. "The cost to an organization of an original one-page letter is estimated at more than $20 when all office expenses are considered," Manning writes. "It is therefore very important to make sure that your letters are professional in content and organization and support your organization."

Often the reward for traditional sales writing is immediate revenue. The reward for business writing that sells is also financial. Studies show that good writers make more money than their grammatically-challenged counterparts. And, as a skilled communicator, you also are likely to receive added prestige, promotions, and visibility in your workplace.

By reading this book and doing the exercises, you will be able to better persuade, motivate, and influence your readers. Each chapter provides lessons on classic sales techniques, and ways to incorporate them into your writing. You'll learn how to personalize your message, counter possible objections, and most important, make your writing *sing*.

Good luck!

Kathleen A. Begley

Contents

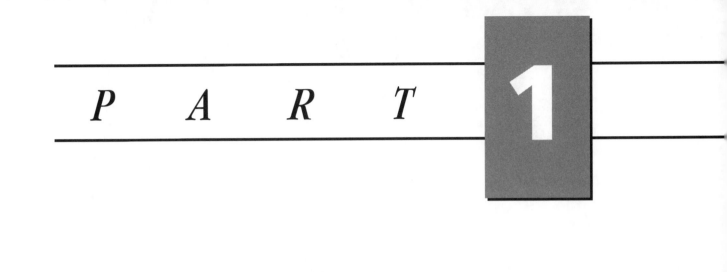

PART 1

Rethink Sales

2

Recognize Your Sales Purpose

You may be a chemical engineer or a mailroom supervisor and never sell actual products or services. After all, that is the marketing department's job. Right? Well, yes and no.

Information technology, administration, finance, manufacturing, and distribution are all engaged in selling. But rather than *tangible* products and services, these departments are pushing *intangible* concepts. Guess which selling job is more difficult? You're right—intangibles.

Persuade, Motivate, Sell

Every e-mail, letter, and proposal you write on the job qualifies as a sales pitch. Think about documents you turn out on a routine basis. Do they merely communicate information with a take-it-or-leave-it attitude? Probably not.

Whether or not you realize it at the time of writing, you may be trying to convince or persuade your readers to:

➤ Approve additions to staff

➤ Implement a telecommuting program

➤ Accept your offer of employment

➤ Participate in the company blood drive

➤ Increase the budget for your department

➤ Improve their performance on the job

➤ Adopt the new safety program

➤ Remain loyal and trusting customers

➤ Support travel to out-of-town conferences

➤ Make an exception to company policy

➤ Accept your research findings or survey results

➤ Feel good about the company

➤ Excuse your error in judgment

Business writers often call the concept persuasive writing—perhaps to avoid tainting themselves with the negative image often applied to sales and sales-people. But the techniques of traditional selling are useful not just for moving actual goods. Writing to sell is as much for you—the non-salesperson—as it is for your company's sales and marketing staff.

As you can see from the above examples and the following exercise, most on-the-job communications have an underlying persuasive—sales—purpose.

IDENTIFY THE WRITER'S GOAL

Read the following document summaries. All have an underlying sales purpose: The writer wants the reader either to take a specific action or to adopt a particular viewpoint. See if you can figure it out.

Write beneath each one what the writer is trying to get the recipient of the communication to do. We have answered the first one for you.

1. Letter of termination to a problem employee

   Desired reader response: *Accept the termination gracefully.*

2. E-mail to employees asking for contributions to charity

   Desired reader response: _____

   _____

3. Memo to managers about elimination of executive parking

   Desired reader response: _____

   _____

4. Report to accounting about travel to a marketing conference in Hawaii

   Desired reader response: _____

   _____

5. Proposal to top management for a 20% personnel increase

   Desired reader response: _____

   _____

6. E-mail to production people inviting them to a sales meeting

   Desired reader response: _____

   _____

7. Letter to a temporary employee offering a permanent job

   Desired reader response: _____

   _____

Compare your answers with the author's suggested responses in the Appendix.

Value the Quick Sale

According to reliable research, salespeople have less than 60 seconds to attract the attention of their prospects. A study conducted in 2001 by Dr. Kim Allen, a sales executive at Astra Zeneca Pharmaceuticals, showed that so-called face time could be as little as six seconds when dealing with extremely busy people such as physicians.

No wonder one strength of successful salespeople is making the most of time—their own and their prospects'.

Write to the Point

As a writer, you also face a time crunch in getting your readers to stop doing what they are doing and focus on your communication. Bluntly put, you need to go for the quick sale.

"Schoolbook grammar is irrelevant in the sales letter," writes Dan Kennedy in *The Ultimate Sales Letter*. "Instead, use every weapon in your arsenal—odd punctuation and phrasing, non-sentences, one-word exclamations, buzzwords—to push and prod and pull the reader along, and to create momentum and excitement."

Momentum? Excitement? Yes, remember that the premise of this book is that although you may not be selling products and services, you are always selling ideas. And you have to make it snappy.

Quick sale is not a negative term. It means that you are showing respect for your prospect's valuable time.

CASE STUDY: COMPARE THESE SALESPEOPLE

Amanda just took a job selling copiers to large companies. Right out of college, she has little experience in business. The person who would normally train her is on paternity leave. On her first week of sales calls, Amanda tried to put into practice something she had read about: creating rapport with clients. When approaching a customer, she commented on everything in the office that lent itself to small talk—photos, diplomas, awards. The trouble was that nearly 20 minutes passed and she still hadn't got around to presenting her product. She caught the prospect looking at his watch several times, and her 30-minute meeting time was about up.

Emily, also a recent college graduate, took a job selling beauty supplies to hair salons. She received two weeks of intense training, which taught her proven sales techniques. Like Amanda, she opened conversations with prospects by chitchatting. But she quickly moved on to describe her shampoos and conditioners, mention their high mark-up potential, explain their superiority over other brands, and ask for the order. She was in and out of every prospect's office in less than 15 minutes.

Who do you think has a better future in sales? Why?

_____

_____

_____

Compare your answers with the author's suggested responses in the Appendix.

Step into Your Readers' Shoes

Having identified Emily as the better salesperson for her effective use of time, apply the same principle to writing. Think like your readers and you know that only so much time is available for miscellaneous communications.

After all, when was the last time you felt overjoyed about seeing a long list of e-mail messages waiting on your computer? Be honest. Don't you feel just a little annoyed by the volume of documents you have to read just to keep up with day-to-day tasks?

Yet, inexplicably, we business writers often act as if readers have nothing better to do than read every long, tedious word of our documents. Come on now. Do you really think that typical readers clap their hands in glee when they receive a communication about a new plant construction on the other side of the country or a recently hired vice president in Amsterdam?

See Your Ideas from Your Readers' Perspective

Most likely, people receiving your messages are doing something else at the time. And they are involved and committed to their own assignment. So your first task as a writer is to learn how to divert people's focus.

Take the advice of Herschell Gordon Lewis, author of *Sales Letters That Sizzle*. "Get to the point," Lewis says. "Don't dawdle. Don't try to be subtle because subtlety will cost you some response. Subtlety suppresses response. Cleverness for the sake of cleverness suppresses response. In-jokes suppress response. Starting in low gear suppresses response. So—get to the point!"

Still unconvinced that thinking like a salesperson will help you write documents such as e-mails about ergonomic issues, letters of resignation, or proposals for new signage? Part 2 will show you how to put sales theory into practice.

ANALYZE YOUR OWN READING BEHAVIOR

Take this brief quiz by answering always, sometimes, or never.

	Always	Sometimes	Never
When I get unexpected e-mail, I immediately drop everything and read the message with great interest.	❏	❏	❏
I have little to do at work other than read and decipher long, overly detailed documents.	❏	❏	❏
Before lunch, I enjoy searching through several pages of a document to try to figure out the overall gist.	❏	❏	❏
It makes me happy when I have to check old correspondence to understand a point in a new proposal.	❏	❏	❏
If a writer fails to include information from my viewpoint, I shrug off the lapse without judgment.	❏	❏	❏
I dislike it when writers use words such as "benefits" or "advantages" to attract my attention.	❏	❏	❏
I always give equal time to every document that comes over my desk.	❏	❏	❏
In a work situation, I see little competition for time, effort, or money.	❏	❏	❏

CONTINUED

CONTINUED

	Always	Sometimes	Never
When I want to move forward on a proposal, I don't mind spending extra time looking up full names, phone numbers, and addresses necessary to take action.	❏	❏	❏
It annoys me when a writer gives me a variety of options, such as a choice of replying in hard copy or by e-mail.	❏	❏	❏

Compare your answers with the author's suggested responses in the Appendix.

Part 1 Summary

Put a check (✔) in the box next to ideas you intend to use in your next writing project:

❑ Recognize the sales objective of all business documents.

❑ Understand a common purpose of salespeople and writers: a quick sale.

❑ See your ideas from your readers' perspective.

Use the S.A.L.E.S.

Model

" Some of the sharpest traders we know are artists, and
some of the best salesmen are writers."

–journalist E.B. White

14

Write to Sell with a Five-Step Formula

Converting classic sales principles into persuasive writing is what this book is all about. Whether you are selling widgets to customers or proposing a new company policy to the board of directors, you need to follow the same five-step S.A.L.E.S. model:

Start by getting your readers' attention

Add the background essentials and unique features

List the benefits from your readers' viewpoint

Evaluate and counter possible objections

Sign off with an either/or call to action

Each of the steps in this model forms a kind of sales checklist. There is no way to devise an exact formula for every sales situation. When you are writing to sell your idea, run through the S.A.L.E.S. model first. With effort and practice, this new approach to persuasive writing will become automatic.

Start by Getting Your Readers' Attention

You are undoubtedly familiar with this technique as a consumer. Consider, for example, the perfume or cologne saleswoman who asks permission to spray your wrist as you walk through a department store. Why not project this attention-grabbing concept into written documents by asking questions, making startling statements, or referring to an earlier encounter?

"How would you like improved healthcare coverage, less paperwork, and faster prescription reimbursements? Well, it's about to become a reality!"

Add the Background Essentials and Unique Features

Advertisements for products as varied as running shoes and eyeglasses carry details about who should use them, what the products are made from, when they will be available, where they can be bought, and why they are better than other similar products. As a writer reaching out to readers, you will become more effective by thinking through the same five Ws (what, who, when, where, and why) to sell your ideas.

"On Friday, October 15, our employee benefits manager will be here to explain the new health-care plan, which become effective on November 1."

List Benefits from Your Readers' Viewpoint

"Benefits, benefits, benefits" is the mantra of salespeople. Fast food is popular not because low-paid personnel save owners money but because drive-through windows save customers time. The lesson: Be sure to present arguments from your readers' viewpoint, not your own.

"Topics to be covered include why this plan was selected, how it will save you time and money, and what impact it will have on your choice of doctors and other healthcare providers."

Evaluate and Counter Possible Objections

Sales trainers often encourage new hires to speculate about what prospects might say to get out of buying. This technique is called anticipating objections. Good sales training gives professionals ways of countering negative comments about products as diverse as microwave ovens, ski gear, down comforters, dental implants, and walking sticks. Similarly, you should pre-think all possible objections to the ideas you want to express in your e-mails, letters, and proposals.

"I know you are all very busy, but I have been told by other organizations that the hour is well worth our time—packed with information you will want to know and complete handouts on the plan. The presenter will also answer individual questions during the session."

Sign Off with an Either/Or Call to Action

The assumptive close is well known in sales circles. At the end of a pitch about computer training, for example, experienced customer service representatives steadfastly avoid asking whether or not you want to register for a class. Instead, they ask whether you prefer classroom or e-learning, short-term immersion or long-term curricula, college credits or continuing education units. As a writer, you should also dream up alternatives available to your readers.

"Sessions will be offered at 11:00 A.M. and 3:00 P.M. Please let me know by the end of day tomorrow which session you plan to attend."

CASE STUDY: TRADITIONAL SALES AT WORK

The following is an example of a classic sales scenario: an encounter between salespeople and customers in an electronics store. See if you can identify where the salespeople cover every step in the S.A.L.E.S. model.

Put yourself in the shoes of Chris and Lee who are shopping for a big-screen television capable of receiving hundreds of channels in the comfort of their home. In the electronics store, you approach a huge bank of TVs, all tuned to a major sports event.

So what do savvy salespeople do? Ask which team you're rooting for, of course. The object is to attract your attention and get you involved.

But Lee looks totally uninterested in the game in progress. Now what do experienced salespeople do? They instantly switch gears and point out that the TV also pulls in a wealth of family entertainment, special-interest programming, and educational fare. Can you say Shakespeare?

When Chris and Lee are both intrigued, good salespeople enumerate the essential facts: what channels the TV gets, who makes it, when it can be shipped, where you can get service, and why you should own one. And, oh yes, if at all possible, clever salespeople will try to get you to use the remote control or handle the on-off switch. Isn't it fascinating that marketing folks understood interactivity long before computer developers did?

Ah, but Chris and Lee are still acting unsure. Perceptive salespeople notice a grimace here, exchanged glances there. So then they launch into a long list of benefits you will get from buying the TV, the faster the better. It is on sale. It comes with free delivery. It is the latest technology. How on earth could you possibly keep up with the Joneses without one?

Lee mentions that you have unusually high expenses right now. You need a new refrigerator. Your daughter is getting braces. You may lose your job. Not to worry, fast-thinking sales types say. Refrigerators are on sale too. You usually can pay the orthodontist over time. And if you do lose your job, wouldn't you like to spend your extra time watching this fabulous TV?

And then it is time for the so-called kill. Salespeople call it closing the deal. Rather than asking a "yes" or "no" question about whether you want to buy the TV, they offer options:

"Do you want the model in mahogany or oak?"

"Would you like to take it with you today or have it delivered tomorrow?"

"Are you going to pay cash or put the purchase on an easy installment plan?"

The idea is to get you over the hump of whether or not you want to buy—and encourage you to decide on details. What are the odds that Chris and Lee will buy?

RECOGNIZE THE S.A.L.E.S. TECHNIQUE

Now review the sales presentation and answer the following questions:

1. How did the salespeople get Chris' and Lee's attention?

_____

_____

2. What background essentials and unique advantages were pointed out?

_____

_____

3. What benefits were presented?

_____

_____

4. How did the salespeople evaluate and counter objections?

_____

_____

5. What kind of sign-off was used?

_____

_____

Compare your answers with the author's suggested responses in the Appendix.

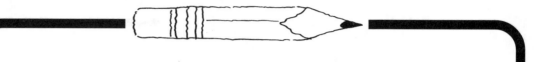

THE S.A.L.E.S. MODEL IN WRITING

The five-part S.A.L.E.S. model can be applied in written communication the same as in a classic face-to-face sales presentation, as you will see in the e-mail message below. Write the meaning of each letter of the S.A.L.E.S. acronym. Then, using this completed model as a memory device, circle the word in the sample e-mail below where the writer begins each step and label it with the appropriate letter.

S _____

A _____

L _____

E _____

S _____

Sample E-mail

```
To: Bridget Sheppard
From: Jason Harvey
Date: July 18, 2002
Subject Line: Thank you for the great ideas!

Bridget,

You really helped me today with your terrific ideas. Thanks to
you, I think the new advertising campaign for The Superb Com-
pany—while expensive—will succeed beyond expectations when it
debuts next month in national media. Bridget, you're a valuable
member of our team; I know you'll advance far in this company
because of your willingness to share your creativity. I really
appreciate your taking time out from your busy schedule today
to do lunch. If I can help you in any way, please give me a
call at 555-7777 or send me an e-mail reply.

Jason
```

Compare your answers with the author's suggested responses in the Appendix.

Choose the More Persuasive Sentence

Imagine you are the community relations manager for The Awesome Company. To improve its community image, the firm is volunteering for a mentoring program. You need to draft a letter to all employees about teaming up with low-income youths between the ages of eight and 12.

Choose which of the two sentences in each example below would better achieve your purpose. Circle the letter of your selection.

1. Start by Getting Your Readers' Attention

A. The Awesome Company is starting a new mentoring program.

B. The Awesome Company wants you! And so do dozens of low-income, inner-city children who need mentors to help them on the road to success.

2. Add the Background Essentials and Unique Features

A. Begun by President Jane Brooks, The Awesome Company mentoring program—a first in the city—will kick off at noon Friday at headquarters.

B. The mentoring program is being started by Jane this week.

3. List the Benefits from Your Readers' Viewpoint

A. The Awesome Company wants to be known in the community for its good works.

B. As a mentor, you'll feel great sharing your knowledge with a young person who truly needs you.

4. Evaluate and Counter Possible Objections

A. We know you'll want to do this.

B. Pressed for time? Aren't we all? But isn't one hour a week a small price to pay for the satisfaction of knowing you're contributing positively to our community?

CONTINUED

22

5. Sign Off with an Either/Or Call to Action

A. You may respond either by hard copy or e-mail or by calling 555-1111 or 555-2222.

B. If you want to participate, please call 555-3333.

Compare your answers with the author's suggested responses in the Appendix.

Start by Getting Your Readers' Attention

Attempts to get your attention abound in everyday life. TV commercials for laundry detergent become louder than the programming. Web sites for children's toys use animated banners to draw your eye to featured products. Billboards touting icy beer use bigger-than-life photographs. Yet many writers think their ideas are so powerful that they can skip the attention-getting step. Wrong. Avoid falling into this trap by making your subject lines and first sentences especially powerful.

In her book, *Better Business Writing,* Susan Brock says the purpose of the opening or attention-getting part of a document is to overcome the inevitable "reader apathy" to any new idea. Here are five ways to do it:

Ask a Question

Not: To attract young professionals to its staff, The First Company has installed showers in its restrooms.

But: How would you like to be able to take a shower after doing your three-mile fitness run at lunch? You could if you worked at The First Company.

Use the Word "You"

Not: Direct deposit will save money for The Progressive Company.

But: You'll have immediate access to your money on payday thanks to the new direct deposit system here at The Progressive Company.

Make a Startling Statement

Not: Sales are low in the restaurant industry.

But: Overall sales in the restaurant industry have fallen 37% since September, the largest three-month decline since the recession of 1981.

Refer to a Personal Fact

Not: I received your letter of Jan. 16 regarding additional parts for your auto body shop.

But: I enjoyed having lunch with you the last time you were in town. Thanks for your recent order of additional parts for your auto body shop.

Quote Well-Recognized Persons

Not: Success in this program depends on attending all the sessions.

But: Woody Allen once said, "Eighty percent of success is showing up."

HOOK YOUR READER

Pretend you are a manager in the Human Resources (HR) department of The Cash Company, a financial services company that has major offices in New York, Los Angeles, Beijing, Singapore, Bangalore, and London. Nigel Whitethorn, the HR vice president, has asked you to recruit 12 members for a cross-functional committee to develop a new policy for rewarding people who provide beyond-the-call-of-duty customer service. The impetus for the change has been a growing number of complaints from many of the organization's 100,000 employees about a lack of recognition of their contribution to the firm's success. Your vice president wants the new committee to spend six months preparing a soup-to-nuts report into reward policies in other major global corporations. Among items to be considered are criteria, fairness, and value of the awards. The vice president is convinced that recognizing excellence is a key to retaining good people and continuing growth. Committee members will meet in each of the main offices, starting in New York with an introductory session and ending in London with publication of recommendations.

Possible Techniques:

➤ Ask a question.

➤ Use the word "you."

➤ Make a startling statement.

➤ Refer to a personal fact.

➤ Quote well-recognized persons.

Your opening statement(s):

_____

_____

Compare your answers with the author's suggested responses in the Appendix.

Add the Background Essentials and Unique Features

In classic sales, it is easy to pick out distinctions between your product and the next guy's. Your computer runs faster than the others. Your paper is less expensive than your competitor's. Your home repair service has been in business longer than anyone else in town.

In *Spend Less, Sell More,* author David Rosenweig says salespeople must be able to point out "distinctive capabilities, which are those abilities that set your company apart from the competition."

It is critical to do the same thing when describing ideas in writing. You have to give readers a reason they should devote time and energy to your communication rather than to all the other piles of information on their desk or in their computer. Start with the basic facts. Then emphasize the unique advantage of your idea.

The Five Ws

An easy way to think through this step of the sales-writing process is to identify the five Ws as they apply to your idea:

➤ What is the idea?

➤ Who is involved?

➤ When will it take effect?

➤ Where will it take place?

➤ Why should your readers care about this idea?

Let's say you want your employer, The Bountiful Company, to permit employees to bring their dogs to work. You have tentatively named your idea "K-9-2-5." You are writing a brief proposal to the executive committee. Your answers to the five Ws might be as follows:

What: *to permit Bountiful Company employees to bring their dogs to work on Fridays*

Who: *about 100 hourly and salaried people—76% of whom have pets*

When: *about 90 days after an official e-mail announcement*

Where: *at Bountiful Company headquarters*

Why: *because K-9-2-5 will show employees that the company cares about their emotional well-being and connectedness to their pets. As a result, the innovative policy might inspire increased loyalty and productivity.*

DESCRIBE THE BIG PICTURE

Continue with the memo about recruitment of the cross-functional committee to make recommendations regarding customer service awards at The Cash Company. Describe the five Ws and unique features of the idea.

Possible Techniques:

➤ What

➤ Who

➤ When

➤ Where

➤ Why

Your background paragraph:

_____

_____

_____

_____

Compare your answers with the author's suggested responses in the Appendix.

List Benefits from Your Readers' Viewpoint

"Benefits" is a household term to well-trained salespeople. They know the secret to selling toothpaste is not to list its chemical ingredients, but to point out the sex appeal of fresh breath. Let's face it. The average consumer could care less that toothpaste contains technical sounding ingredients such as sodium monofluorophosphate.

Marilyn Ross, author of *Brazen Marketing for Shameless Hussies,* advises, "When you emphasize benefits, you tell the customer/client what she or he will get: not what your product or service is, but what it does. Features tell what it is. Benefits tell prospects what's in it for them."

Appeal to Human Needs

Savvy salespeople recognize that most 21st-century consumers are short on two things: time and money. Among the top needs that motivate people to buy, then, are making or saving money and saving time. But they are not the only ones.

Consider Starbucks Coffee Company. Chairman and CEO Howard Schultz says he came to realize, as time went on, that there was more to the company's success than a better cup of coffee. In his book, *Pour Your Heart into It,* Schultz writes: "We realized that our stores had a deeper resonance and were offering benefits as seductive as the coffee itself." Among them, he says:

➤ A taste of romance

➤ An affordable luxury

➤ An oasis from the fast-paced world

➤ Casual social interaction

Relate the Benefits to Your Reader

Just as Schultz stepped back and recognized that his customers' perceptions about Starbucks were different from his own, writers at the benefits stage must do the same thing. As human beings, we are often so locked into our own thoughts that we are slow to relate to others' needs.

Say you are composing a letter to your manager, asking for a 10% raise. Obviously, what *you* are most interested in is making more money. But what is in it for your manager? Focus on the benefits the manager might accrue in giving you the raise. The following examples show the difference between aiming your message at the recipient (your manager) rather than the sender (you).

Make Money

Not: I want a raise so I can buy a bigger house.

But: A 10% raise will make me 100% happier and more productive on the job.

Save Time

Not: Getting a raise here would save me the time of having to look for a new job elsewhere.

But: A raise would convince me to stay at this job, which would save you the time of finding and training a replacement.

Provide Safety and Security

Not: I need more money for my financial security.

But: If I get a raise, I won't have to disrupt our team's progress.

Enhance a Sense of Belonging

Not: I hope to retire from this company.

But: A pay increase would convince me to stay a loyal member of your team.

Help Readers Achieve Their Potential

Not: If I get a raise, I hope to go back to school and get my master's degree.

But: If I get a raise, I will do everything I can to help you maintain your reputation as a first-rate supervisor.

TELL READERS WHAT'S IN IT FOR THEM

Return to The Cash Company memo. Step into your readers' shoes as you enumerate the benefits of serving on the committee regarding customer service rewards.

➤ Achieving more comfort

➤ Having better health

➤ Escaping pain

➤ Gaining praise

➤ Being loved and accepted

➤ Seeking more enjoyment

➤ Satisfying curiosity

➤ Protecting family

➤ Having beautiful things

➤ Being like others or being individual

➤ Avoiding trouble or criticism

➤ Protecting reputation

➤ Seizing opportunity

➤ Being safe and secure

➤ Making work easier

Your Benefits Paragraph:

_____

_____

_____

Compare your answers with the author's suggested responses in the Appendix.

Evaluate and Counter Possible Objections

The trickiest part of most real-life sales calls is uncovering unspoken, but very real, objections. Many prospects will not say, for example, that they lack the money to buy your product. Similarly, your readers may not be authorized to give the final say-so on your idea. So you need to anticipate all possibilities.

In a lengthy chapter about selling in *Start Your Own Business,* author Rieva Lesonsky says salespeople often counter objections about time and money by showing that customers get "more services, better warranties, or higher quality products for the extra cost."

But there are many other possible objections besides those concerned with time and money. When you are trying to make a persuasive argument in business, objections are most often centered on five concerns:

➤ Fears

➤ Resentments

➤ Adequate planning

➤ The manager's reaction

➤ Safety net or bail-out option

Let's take a look at each possible objection as it relates to persuading your manager to accomplish weekend work with temporary contractors only, not with company employees. Following are some wrong and right ways of overcoming these objections.

Bring Up Fears

Not: Customers will never know they're not talking to a real employee.

But: If you're concerned about less coverage by employees, put away your worries. We've taken a survey of other departments and companies and found that many have made the same switch. A decrease in customer satisfaction has never been indicated.

Address Possible Resentment

Not: It really doesn't matter what contractors think of the plan.

But: During our planning, we discussed possible resentment on the part of the contractors about having to work weekends. Then we surveyed a number of these independent workers. Everyone we spoke to was eager to get more hours any time, even on the weekends.

Show That You Have Thought the Plan Through

Not: Our customer service responsiveness will not be affected.

But: To ward off even the slim possibility of inferior service, we've built into the plan a special training session for weekend workers.

Give Co-Workers an Explanation for Their Managers

Not: I wouldn't worry about what your bosses think.

But: Let's face it. Managers may have some anxiety about this change. So we've provided a fact sheet to show your bosses how this idea has paid off in other companies.

Build in a Safety Net

Not: It's a foolproof plan.

But: If something happens to go wrong, you can always point the finger at us. We feel confident you'll never get to that point.

ANSWER OBJECTIONS BEFORE THEY COME UP

Go back to the memo about recruitment for the cross-functional committee asked to spend six months developing a new policy regarding customer service awards. Answer possible objections readers may have to spending so much time on this issue.

Techniques for Overcoming Objections:

➤ Bring up fears

➤ Address possible resentments

➤ Show that you have thought the plan through

➤ Give co-workers an explanation for their managers

➤ Build in a safety net

Your counter paragraph:

_____

_____

_____

Compare your answers with the author's suggested responses in the Appendix.

Sign Off with an Either/Or Call to Action

According to Robert W. Bly, author of *Selling Your Services,* inexperienced salespeople often forget to make a call to action. So they do not sell much. As a writer, you will fail to get approval for your ideas unless you similarly make a call to action. Even in brief e-mails, you have to close the sale.

You must "tell readers the specific action you want them to take and spell out the benefits they will receive if they respond now," Bly writes. In writing, you can end your document with any of these techniques:

Give a Choice of Phone Numbers

Not: Call me at 555-4444.

But: Please call me with any questions at 555-1234 or 555-4321.

Suggest Several Ways to Respond

Not: Reply to my e-mail by Oct. 13.

But: Reply by Oct. 13 by e-mail, hard copy, or phone call.

Provide Meeting Options

Not: The meeting is scheduled at 10 A.M. Thursday.

But: You can find out more about the changes by attending a meeting at 10 A.M. Thursday or 4 P.M. Friday.

Break a Day into Halves

Not: I can be reached Thursday.

But: You can reach me either Thursday morning or Thursday afternoon.

List a Range of Follow-up Contacts

Not: For more information, hit the reply button.

But: For more information, hit the reply button to reach me or call my assistant Margo Shelby.

ASK READERS TO TAKE ACTION

Finish the memo about The Cash Company customer service awards. Be specific about action you want your readers to take in response to your request.

Possible Techniques:

➤ Give a choice of phone numbers.

➤ Suggest different ways to respond.

➤ Provide meeting options.

➤ Break a day into halves.

➤ List a range of follow-up contacts.

Your sign-off:

_____

_____

_____

_____

_____

_____

Compare your answers with the author's suggested responses in the Appendix.

DISSECT THIS DOCUMENT

To reinforce your learning, once again fill out the meaning of each initial in the S.A.L.E.S. model below. Then read the proposal that follows, which demonstrates the technique in a longer, more complex fashion than the earlier e-mail exercise. Circle the word where the writer starts each part of the five-part selling process and label it with the appropriate letter of the S.A.L.E.S. model.

S_____

A_____

L_____

E_____

S_____

Public Relations Proposal

For several decades, The Overlooked Company has spent more than $100 million annually in paid advertising of its mail-order contact lenses. It has poured this money into conventional media, including national magazines and network television.

Unfortunately, Overlooked has received little return on its promotional budget. We at Powerful Public Relations think we know why and how to change the situation.

This proposal is for a yearlong, first-time-ever effort to increase Overlooked's name recognition by attracting press coverage in carefully selected media rather than placing paid advertising. Estimated to cost $12 million, the campaign targets 21- to 35-year-old women, who make up Overlooked's key market.

CONTINUED

Designed as an add-on to paid advertising, Powerful Public Relations' plan will involve lobbying print, broadcast, and cable reporters and editors for inclusion in editorial stories rather than in orchestrated ads. According to studies by the Public Relations Society of America, an industry trade group, consumers tend to read editorial content more readily than they do ads. And they tend to believe seemingly independent media coverage at a higher level than clearly controlled commercial messages.

The benefits for Overlooked are clear. At slightly more than 10% of the current advertising budget, the firm will:

➤ Get its message to people who don't read or look at advertisements.

➤ Obtain the appearance of third-party endorsement by the news media.

➤ Reap the benefits of a combined advertising/public relations campaign.

Yes, although public relations is inexpensive compared to paid ads, $10 million still is a sizable amount of money. And, without a doubt, publicity seekers have much less control over the message and timing of editorial stories than they do over placed advertisements. But the payoff such as a front-page story in the *New York Times* or a five-minute spot on CNN is incalculable. You literally cannot buy this kind of placement.

We at Powerful Public Relations would like to set up a meeting next week to present you with details of our plan. We can schedule that on Thursday or Friday. Which would be better for you? Please contact us at 555-3784 or we will call you to arrange.

Compare your answers with the author's suggested responses in the Appendix.

SELL YOUR OWN IDEA

Now it is your turn to try your hand with the S.A.L.E.S. model. Think of a challenge you currently face in which you want to convince someone to adopt your idea, use your services, or even buy your product. A cover letter on a job application is one possibility. Or you may want to practice by writing a memo pushing for purchase of a new computer system.

Select an idea for the entire document. Fill in the outline. A hint: To get you started, leap into the middle or the end rather than the beginning.

Start by getting your readers' attention.

_____

_____

Add the background essentials and unique features.

_____

_____

List benefits from your readers' viewpoint.

_____

_____

Evaluate and counter possible objections.

_____

_____

Sign off with an either/or option for taking action.

_____

_____

Compare your answers with the author's suggested responses in the Appendix.

Part 2 Summary

Put a check (✔) in the box next to ideas you intend to use in your next
writing project:

❑ Understand the five-step S.A.L.E.S. model and its application to writing.

❑ Hook your readers with an attention-getting opener.

❑ Describe the five Ws to explain your viewpoint.

❑ Appeal to your readers' needs to sell them on your idea.

❑ Answer objections before they come up.

❑ Ask readers to take action.

40

Involve Your

Readers' Senses

Anything that won't sell, I don't want to invent. Its sale is proof of utility and utility is success."

—inventor Thomas Edison

Understand Sensory Styles

As you learned from the S.A.L.E.S. model outlined in Part 2, persuading readers to your viewpoint starts with getting your readers' attention. Then, as you address the background essentials, benefits, and possible objections, you will be better able to keep your readers' attention if you appeal to their *sensory style*.

People receive and transmit information primarily through their senses of sight, touch, and hearing. Thus, their sensory style is labeled visual, tactile, and auditory, respectively. People generally exercise a mix of all three styles, but most will show a dominant preference for one sensory style over the others.

Visual (Sight)

The majority of human beings are especially tuned in to their sense of sight. Across cultures, people have become accustomed to the optical stimulus of movies, television, and advertising. Visual readers often use expressions such as "Looks fabulous!" or "I see what you mean."

People who are predominately *visual* may ask you to put it in writing, send them an e-mail, or mail them a brochure. They often want time to look over information and prepare a response based on what they *see*.

Tactile (Touch)

Some individuals are touchy-feely types. These people relate well to details such as textures and smoothness. They can be identified by their conversational use of words such as "soft," "rough," and "grainy."

Tactile learners often prefer to interact with a product, an idea, a concept. They may want to see a model, ask you to send them a sample, or request a site visit. People with this sensory style may seek tangible evidence before making a decision.

Auditory (Hearing)

The third group listens closely. They pay attention to sound in most situations. You can identify them by their statements such as "I hear you" and "Sounds great."

Auditory sensors are generally comfortable simply discussing an idea, either in person or over the telephone. People who favor this style may enjoy a presentation, a discussion over lunch, spontaneous hallway discussions, or lively debates. They tend to process in the moment and may be able to come to conclusions quickly.

Applying Sensory Style to Sales and Persuasion

In selling products and services, savvy salespeople tailor their pitches to the perceived sensory preference of their prospects. And when you write to sell, you can adapt the same techniques to fit the writing context.

If your appeal is to a single reader whose style you have identified, you can address your message to suit that style. More often, however, the audience for your written communication will be a mix of styles so you will need to appeal to all three styles.

Make It Look Good
(for the Visual Reader)

Visual appeal on paper can be compared to principles of interior design. Just as you have to plan the structure, traffic flow, and focal point in a room arrangement, so too must you allow for similar elements in the written pieces you prepare. The following tips will help you make the best use of the graphics capability of your word processing or desktop design software.

Leave White Space

Not: Put text and graphics on every inch of the paper.

But: Leave enough space unsullied by ink to permit the eyeball to move around the page the way a person would be able to move among—and not have to crawl over—pieces of furniture in a well-designed room.

Play Up a Dominant Element

Not: Use visuals in the same size as all the others.

But: Blow up one or two visuals larger than the rest. This principle of graphic dominance is parallel to the common decorating practice of using a sofa with two chairs rather than four same-size chairs.

Border Text and Graphics

Not: Let information float without any directional lines.

But: Direct readers' eyes inward to important parts of the document with graphic borders. These serve a purpose similar to the walls of a room.

Arrange Parallel Items into Bulleted Lists

Not: Use long, gray paragraphs of unbroken prose.

But: Break key points into separate bullets, much the way you might arrange distinct photographs on a wall rather than making one huge collage.

Use Headings as Guideposts

Not: Skip headings because they take up too much space.

But: Insert headings to help readers get their bearings. Retail interior designers do this by putting up signs telling customers the location of specific products.

Appeal to the Touch (for the Tactile Reader)

Just as new-car salespeople always invite you to sit in the car and get a feel of the upholstery, you can take advantage of the human need for touch to heighten interest in your writing. Think of textural elements that match the message you are wanting to convey.

Splurge on Textured Paper

Not: Print an environmental notice on bleached white copy paper.

But: Put the notice on textured recycled paper; note explicitly that the ink is soy-based.

Consider Dimensional Printing

Not: Send invitations to the 10th anniversary conference printed in flat black ink.

But: Use dimensional printing techniques such as embossing and gold lettering for unusually festive occasions.

Design Creative Die Cuts

Not: Prepare standard invitations to the annual meeting in Atlanta, Georgia, and fit them into a basic business envelope.

But: Print the invitations on pinkish tan cover stock and then bulk cut the cards into the shape of a peach–Georgia's trademark fruit.

Insert Lumpy Enclosures

Not: Make sure all envelopes are completely flat to ensure machine handling.

But: Obtain permission from your mail carrier to send envelopes containing a giveaway such as an eraser, Post-It note pad, or candy bar–a surefire attention getter.

Become a Heavyweight

Not: Send all mail on lightweight paper to show fiscal responsibility.

But: Use dense, high quality paper stock when sending notices about high-end stocks, luxury cars, or gala events.

Make Your Writing Sing (for the Auditory Reader)

On the face of it, appealing to the sense of hearing while writing seems odd. But sound conveys messages on paper as well as on musical instruments.

Alliterate Always (Okay, Sometimes)

Not: The manager is hard driving.

But: The manager is driven, demanding, and decisive.

Use Creative Word Plays

Not: In every way, I care for you all the time.

But: Always, in all ways, I care for you.

Make Reason with Rhymes

Not: Apples make you healthy.

But: An apple a day keeps the doctor away.

Have Fun with Words That Sound Like Their Meanings

Not: The truck encountered wet snow.

But: The truck encountered slush.

Repeat, but Only Effectively

Not: We must stop terrorism for posterity.

But: We must stop terrorism for the sake of our children, for the sake of their children, and for the sake of their children's children.

Make It Visual, Tactile, or Auditory

Imagine that you are trying to convince three different types of readers to attend monthly safety meetings at The Dangerous Company, which manufactures explosives. List the elements in specified categories that might help encourage different types of sensors to accept this call to action:

Visual (Sight)

Words: _____

Sentences: _____

Graphics: _____

Enclosures: _____

Packaging: _____

Tactile (Touch)

Words: _____

Sentences: _____

Graphics: _____

Enclosures: _____

Packaging: _____

Auditory (Hearing)

Words: _____

Sentences: _____

Graphics: _____

Enclosures: _____

Packaging: _____

Compare your answers with the author's suggested responses in the Appendix.

Size Up Your Readers' Personality

In addition to sensory preferences, human beings have distinct preferences about the amount and type of information they like to receive on any given topic. There are four distinct types:

Romantics like a lot of detail with content involving people and feelings.

Entertainers prefer a brief overview with emphasis on fun and interactivity.

Analyticals respond well to long documents filled with facts and figures.

Drivers love brief reports and summaries emphasizing the bottom line.

To get readers to do what you want, it's helpful to send messages in their preferred style. But how do you figure it out? Use the R.E.A.D. Quiz, on the following pages.

To determine your own reading style, take the 10-item quiz yourself. Then, the next time you're communicating to specific individuals, either ask them to take the quiz or guesstimate their answers. With people whom you've met, you can often figure out their preferences by thinking about past interactions. The results also hold well on groups of readers, such as mechanical engineers or video producers, who probably share characteristics that led them to their occupations.

The R.E.A.D. Quiz

To take the quiz, simply circle one answer in each of the 10 questions. There are four possible answers per question. While none of the suggestions may exactly match your thinking, please force yourself to choose the response closest to your personality and behavior. You must circle only one number in each of the 10 items to get an accurate score; you also must answer all 10 questions.

Question 1: When reading a formal letter from someone with whom you have a pleasant telephone-only relationship, you would prefer to be addressed by:

1. Courtesy title such as Mr., Mrs., or Ms.

2. Nickname

3. Academic degree such as "Dr."

4. First name

Question 2: As a reader, you would describe yourself as:

1. Very aware of politeness and courtesy

2. Appreciative of witty writing

3. Interested in evidence supporting arguments

4. Want writers to cut to the chase

Question 3: If you received a 300-page report on a topic on which you were expecting 30 pages, your immediate reaction might be:

1. I'll take this report home and read it over the weekend.

2. I don't have time to read this now, but I will right before the meeting.

3. I'm really impressed by depth of this report.

4. There had better be an executive summary.

CONTINUED

Question 4: A money-related term you relate well to is:

1. Financial security

2. Cash

3. Monetary compensation

4. Bottom line

Question 5: To you, the value of colorful pie charts and bar graphics in business documents is:

1. Increased understanding of complex issues

2. Graphic relief in boring documents

3. Helpful if scientifically sound

4. Easy to grasp, especially on profit and loss issues

Question 6: Your resume contains action verbs most similar to which of the following lists:

1. Encouraged, supported, facilitated

2. Motivated, sold, negotiated

3. Correlated, analyzed, studied

4. Drove, raised, won

Question 7: When given a writing assignment at work, your first act would mostly likely be to:

1. Gather resources and information.

2. Talk about the assignment with co-workers.

3. Outline or diagram the writing task.

4. Get started and get it over.

Question 8: Thinking back to the best business communications class you ever had, the best word to describe your experience would be:

1. Inspired and motivated

2. Entertained and intrigued

3. Interested in techniques and standards

4. Impatient to finish

Question 9: You think many business meetings and presentations you have to attend are:

1. Filled with too much conflict

2. A bit boring and slow moving

3. Too brief to cover topics in depth

4. Overly focused on achieving consensus

Question 10: In your personal life, you enjoy reading:

1. Historical fiction

2. Humor books

3. Scientific reports

4. Autobiographies of business leaders

Scoring the R.E.A.D. Quiz

Now count the number of times you chose answer #1. Then go back and do the same with the other three numbers. Record your numbers here:

1. _____   3. _____

2. _____   4. _____

The line with the highest number indicates your dominant reading style, as described below.

1. **R**omantic Style: Romantic readers are poets at heart, even when dealing with business documents. They often work in helping professions such as nursing or customer service. Their strength is their willingness to look at details and consider all sides of an issue. Their weakness is that they are sometimes slow to make decisions.

2. **E**ntertaining Style: These readers fit well in today's fast-paced, high-tech age. Many trainers and entertainers are in this category. Their strength is an ability to find humor in the most tedious situations. Their weakness is a desire to be entertained even when reading serious, complex business documents.

3. **A**nalytical Style: These readers often come from science and computer backgrounds. In general, they're comfortable working alone for long periods of time. Their strength is precision and accuracy. Their weakness as readers can be a habit of harshly judging more intuitive styles of writing.

4. **D**river Style: These readers fill the executive suits of international companies. Their strength as readers is an ability to zero in   on pertinent business facts. Their weakness is a tendency to become impatient with overly detailed communication.

In this quiz, there is no right or wrong style. The trick is to understand your preference and benefit from its strengths and minimize its weaknesses. When writing to people known to have sensory styles and preferences different from you, it's often wise to downplay your style and flex your message toward your readers' preferences. An example: An entertaining style trying to sell an idea to an analytic reader might want to use less humor and more statistics.

TRANSLATE THIS DOCUMENT

You are a customer service representative for a global telecommunications company. Your manager, who has a romantic reading style, has written a letter responding to a customer's e-mailed complaint about poor service. Aware that readers differ in preferences, your manager has asked you to review and revise the document to appeal to the customer, who based on the style of his e-mail, has a driver preference.

Romantic Style

```
May 8
Michael Lee
The High Tech Company
123 Silicon Blvd.
Palo Alto, CA
```

My Very Dear Mr. Lee,

Please be advised that The Global Telecommunications Company has received your correspondence of April 9, and it has been decided to respond to your concerns pursuant to our core belief in ameliorating unpleasant customer experiences post haste, i.e., avoiding prolonged and protracted conflict of any time with our customers. The Global Telecommunications Company, therefore, desires to extend to The High Tech Company its most sincere and abject apology regarding the poor service that was duly reported to us by you in your last missive. Since registering your complaint in our company records, Global attorneys have conducted a thorough investigation of the matter and coalesce in opinion that the employee with whom you had contact did, indeed, fail to measure up to the high standards of service and courtesy mandated of all company personnel. Although we decline to admit legal culpability in this matter, we want you to know that said employee has been terminated for using profane language when you tried to place an order via telephone and that The High Tech Company will be given three months free services if it chooses to proceed procuring telecommunications networking from this organization.

Very Sincerely Yours,
Olga Katovsky

CONTINUED

How would you rewrite this document?

_____

_____

_____

_____

_____

_____

_____

_____

_____

_____

_____

_____

_____

_____

_____

_____

_____

_____

_____

_____

_____

_____

_____

_____

_____

Part 3 Summary

Put a check (✔) in the box next to ideas that you intend to use in your next writing project:

❑ Understand the value of appealing to your readers' senses.

❑ Build visual appeal into your writing.

❑ Be creative in making your documents touchable.

❑ Read your writing aloud to test for sound appeal.

❑ Adjust your writing style to suit your readers.

Adapt Additional Sales Techniques

" *Kodak sells film, but they don't advertise film. They advertise memories.*"

—educator Theodore Levitt

58

Make It Easy for Readers to Buy

In addition to using the S.A.L.E.S. model and appealing to readers' sensory preferences, other classic face-to-face sales techniques can be adapted to writing that sells.

The best mindset for writing to persuade is big picture thinking. Know, as successful salespeople do, that people rarely buy for just one reason. Purchasing usually involves a progression of decisions that leads customers to put their names on the dotted line or get the cash out their wallets.

When you are writing to persuade, you can tap into the same techniques that top professional sales people use to lead people toward a purchasing decision:

➤ Prequalify your readers

➤ Personalize your message

➤ Create a relationship

➤ Start high on your request

➤ Offer a package deal

➤ Use testimonials

➤ Offer a pilot program or trial period

➤ Establish a sense of urgency

➤ Deliver what you promised

➤ Show gratitude

➤ Be positively persistent

In this section, you will learn how to make these ideas work in your writing. You will discover how specific words, phrases, and sentences can encourage your readers to buy what you are selling—whether it is a concrete product or an abstract idea.

Prequalify Your Readers

Before you broadcast your idea to everyone you can think of, take the time to consider who is really qualified to buy, buy-in, or make a decision. You are wasting everyone's time if you write to people without the money, inclination, or authority to do what you want.

DO	DON'T
Send the memo only to individuals with authority to give the okay.	Send the memo to everyone in the company.
"Joe, I'm happy to report that I can provide the office furniture you want for your new corporate headquarters at an even lower cost than we discussed. As the purchasing agent at your firm, you can rest assured that we will provide all the equipment you need within your budget."	"Joe, I'm unsure if you are the person with the money, but I thought I'd send you this estimate on office furnishings."
"According to the goals you outlined for next year, one of your priorities is to provide increased capability for online communications."	"I would like to talk about an idea for our computer network you may or may not be interested in."
"As vice president of manufacturing, you may want to review my enclosed resume. I recently relocated to San Diego from Philadelphia and would like to talk with you about my 10 years' experience in the same industry. I think there might be a good fit between your company and me."	"I realize you may not be the right person to hire me for a job in manufacturing. But I thought I'd send my resume anyway in case you hear of something in your company."

Personalize Your Message

In this computerized age, there is no excuse for you to fall back on impersonal addresses and salutations. People like to hear their name or read it in writing. Just remember that names probably top the list of places where spelling really counts.

Use available resources to determine the correct form of address for the recipients of your message—particularly in situations involving different cultures and religions. References such as *The New York Times Manual of Style and Usage* are helpful for such nuances. Check the Internet, employee directories, chamber of commerce yearbooks, annual reports, telephone listings, and so on to find exact information.

DO	DON'T
"Dear Mr. Stanton" or "Dear Ms. Friedman."	"To Whom It May Concern" or "Dear Sirs."
Include specific credentials or courtesies when appropriate.	Neglect to include appropriate degrees, titles, and affiliations such as Dr., President, Captain, Pastor.

Create a Relationship

Ask any sales professional what most customers really buy: the product or the salesperson? You guessed it—the human element can make all the difference. Individuals in all walks of life relate more to people than they do to chemical components, manufacturing materials, or technical jargon. That is why top salespeople memorize facts such as their customers' favorite sports, hobbies, and restaurants. Many even save this information in computer programs developed specifically for creating customer profiles.

As a writer, you can borrow this technique by making your readers feel as if they are the only people receiving the message from you. Mass mailings are rarely as effective as one-on-one contacts, so target your appeal to the individual.

DO	DON'T
"You said during my last sales visit that you're always interested in a good deal on office supplies. Have I got a bargain for you! Rashid, you can look like a hero to your cost-conscious boss if you buy these products."	"My company is running its annual sale on office supplies."
"Jennifer, I really enjoyed meeting you at the medical convention last week in Dallas. That Tex-Mex restaurant you took me to was one of the best. Hearing about your adventures in South America was really entertaining."	"It was a pleasure meeting you at the medical convention in Dallas."
"In response to your classified ad in *The Oregonian,* I want to start by saying I think it was unusually clever. Your use of eye-catching graphics certainly got my attention."	"In response to your classified ad in the paper, I think I'm ideal for the job as a graphic designer."

Start High on Your Request

You often can get people to agree to your ideas by using the common negotiating technique of starting out with a high demand—and then scaling back or settling for less. Another form of this technique is to give readers a chance to buy into just a small portion of a larger concept.

DO	DON'T
Ask for more than you expect to receive, then be willing to accept a more realistic outcome.	Start by asking for exactly what you want, leaving yourself with no room for negotiation.
"My preference would be to triple the amount of parking space at headquarters by the end of the year. Based on your feedback about budget constraints, though, I would be happy with doubling it now and tripling it later."	"I guess the only solution for now is to double the amount of parking space."
Lay out a grand plan, then give readers the opportunity to accept in a smaller part of it.	Offer readers all or nothing.
"For a job with so much responsibility, I had expected that my employer would pay 100% of my health benefits. But I'm impressed with the opportunity here, and will be willing to accept 80% coverage with options for improved benefits during contract renewal discussions."	"I won't take a job without 100% of my health benefits paid for by my employer."

Offer a Package Deal

In traditional sales, a package deal involves extending your offer to include more than one product or service. Likewise, when selling ideas, you might create a package by listing various ways the concept will benefit the reader. If your purpose is to sell others on you, then give them a bundle of reasons you are the right person for the job.

DO	DON'T
"When you purchase our training programs, you also get a free needs analysis, exam grading services, certificates of completion, and annual program updates."	"We offer excellent training programs."
"An on-site childcare facility will make it easier for employees with children to stay a bit late when a project needs last-minute attention, will reduce absences due to unreliable childcare arrangements, will make it easier to recruit new employees, and will increase employee loyalty and retention."	"An on-site childcare facility will be of great benefit to our company."
"As a member of your team, I will bring outside perspective, analytical skills, and an established network of proven vendors."	"I will be valuable addition to your team."

Use Testimonials

You should rarely rely only on your own knowledge or opinion to sell your written ideas; get quotes, statistics, and other data to support your position. This technique is similar to what you learned for writing term papers in school: cite passages from books, interview experts, obtain information from people in similar circumstances. Simply stated, you need references to support your case.

DO	DON'T
Obtain quotes from companies where this solution has worked.	Sell an idea based only on your opinion.
"Our travel agency clients have cut airline and hotel costs up to 47%, as verified in the enclosed report."	"Our clients save a lot of money by using our travel agency."
Provide references to substantiate your claims.	Make blanket statements with no offer of proof.
"My clients will tell you that I always meet deadlines. I am enclosing contact information for three that I have worked with throughout the last decade."	"I am prompt and reliable."

Offer a Pilot Program or Trial Period

Readers feel heartened when you acknowledge in your writing that new programs may have kinks that need to be worked out. And you will be more persuasive if your readers know that accepting your proposal will not lock them in forever. They also will appreciate hearing that they will have an opportunity to provide feedback and ideas to improve the product, process, or service.

DO	DON'T
Build in an exit clause or opportunity to re-evaluate the commitment after a certain time period.	Make the decision seem irrevocable.
Start with a pilot program designed to work out unforeseen problems.	Set up a program without opportunity for feedback or revisions.
"Let's kick off the new diversity initiative by doing some pilot training of supervisors on the production floor. That way, we can work out any problems before rolling out the program to the entire corporation."	"Let's sign up all 1,000 employees for this new diversity initiative right away."
Offer a trial period if readers are reluctant to commit long term.	Tell readers they have to make the full commitment or nothing.
"I'm happy to work on a trial contract basis for three months. Then, if you're happy with my work, I would like to become a regular employee."	"I can't take this job unless you can offer me a long-term contract."

Establish a Sense of Urgency

Retailers often run time-specific sales because these encourage customers to close a sale quickly. You can use the same technique in writing. The objective of creating urgency is to prevent your readers from cooling to you, your products, or your ideas after they close your e-mail or toss your memo. You want them to buy what you are selling—right now!

DO	DON'T
Specify a response time frame or a deadline.	Leave the response time open-ended.
"As I mentioned during my visit to your plant, I can give you the sale price on the new heating equipment for your office only until Aug. 15. After that, the equipment will return to original price, which is 35% higher than the pre-season quote."	"Let me know if you want to go ahead with the new heating equipment."
"As I explained during the interview, I have another job offer pending but I would prefer to work with your team. I was very impressed with your organization and the project. If possible, I would appreciate knowing your hiring decision by next Tuesday, as the other company is asking for my decision."	"I'd love to work at your company and look forward to hearing from you."

Deliver What You Promised

Between the sale and delivery of products and services, Murphy's Law—which says that anything that can go wrong, will go wrong—sometimes goes into effect. Orders are lost. Delivery people quit. Products become damaged. The test of a good salesperson is dealing with such crises and keeping the customer happy. A general guideline is that you have to throw in something extra to keep an already disgruntled client in your company's fold.

As a writer, you, too, may have to come to grips with occasional snafus to maintain your reputation for professionalism, expertise, and accuracy.

DO	DON'T
Take responsibility for failings and offer some allowance.	Shirk your responsibility and leave readers hanging.
"I'm sorry we failed to catch the typographical error in our offer. The price is $100 not $10 as my letter said. To make up for any inconvenience, I am going to give you the mistaken price on your initial one-time order."	"Someone failed to proofread the letter I wrote giving you the price you requested. The item you want is $100, not $10."
Spell everything out to head off potential problems.	Expect that problems will take care of themselves.
"To make sure the annual picnic goes smoothly this year, I am enclosing a timeline of all the preparations assigned to specific people."	"If everyone pitches in, the annual picnic should go more smoothly this year."

Show Gratitude

Too many salespeople put most of their effort into winning over hard-to-get prospects—and too little into catering to existing customers. It seems many of us lose sight of the value of people who are already on our side.

Just like customers in the traditional sense, readers have a wide choice of documents to read and concepts to believe in. So whenever you have managed to convince readers of the value of your products and services, ideas, or abilities, show an attitude of gratitude.

DO	DON'T
Be explicit with your appreciation.	Take readers for granted.
"Thank you for placing your recent order for printer cartridges. We value your business."	"We're shipping your cartridge order next week."
"I appreciate all the time and effort you put into considering my idea to repaint all the walls in our office building. Every time I look at the fresh new surroundings, I'll think of you."	"Those dark, dirty walls have needed painting for a long time."
"Thank you for choosing me as your administrative assistant. I can hardly wait to get started."	"I'll see you Monday to start the new job."

Be Positively Persistent

Few customers, or readers, buy anything with one sales pitch or contact. Many sales experts say it takes six to eight communications to sell any product or service which costs more than $100. Keep in mind that you are usually competing with other vendors, employees, and applicants when you are trying to sell something. Avoid a classic selling mistake: giving up too early.

DO	DON'T
Send follow-up e-mail, forward appropriate articles and clippings, take a survey.	Write just one proposal or sales letter and quit after no response.
"I'm following up on my letter of three months ago about the new products we've developed for companies of your size. We just came out with this brochure today and I wanted to make sure you got one hot off the presses."	"I hate to bother you again but here's a new brochure on the products I wrote you about three months ago."
"Building security—this topic seemed of little interest last year when I wrote you a memo about hiring better qualified guards to ensure the safety of our employees and our equipment. In the wake of the crime spree that has run through the warehouse district, I'd like to revisit this issue."	"Well, you certainly blew me off a year ago when I brought up the idea of hiring better qualified security guards. I assume you may want to listen to me now."

PUT IT ALL TOGETHER

You are coaching Renee Gifford, a hard-driving manager at The Major Company. Because her main interest is quarterly profits, she always insists on immediate results. She badgers her staff with never-ending urgent demands.

On Renee's last evaluation, her superiors told her that she needs to develop better communications skills with her 35-member staff. Renee wants to take an e-learning course that she can complete at home in two weekends.

As a training professional, you feel strongly that Renee would benefit more from live classroom interaction. A five-day, interactive class called "People Skills: The Key to Career Success" will be offered at your company's off-site conference center. Write a five-paragraph S.A.L.E.S. memo to Renee using as many techniques as possible from *Writing Persuasively*.

_____

_____

_____

_____

_____

_____

_____

_____

_____

_____

_____

Compare your answers with the author's suggested responses in the Appendix.

Part 4 Summary

Put a check (✔) in the box next to ideas that you intend to use in your next writing project:

- ❑ Write to people with the power to do what you want.

- ❑ Address your message to specific recipients by name.

- ❑ Establish rapport with your readers.

- ❑ Ask for more than what you are willing to settle for.

- ❑ Bundle the benefits of your idea to create a package deal.

- ❑ Create credibility for your concept with others' success stories.

- ❑ Allow for a test run of your idea.

- ❑ Set a deadline to motivate action.

- ❑ Make good on your commitment.

- ❑ Be generous with your thanks to those who adopted your idea.

- ❑ Keep trying to persuade readers to your viewpoint.

Get to the Point

At the moment of a major decision, there's always hesitation. The professional salesperson has to find a way to nudge the prospect past that point."

—motivational speaker Brian Tracy

Go Back to Basics

Just as business travelers prefer the nonstop route, business readers want information transmitted in the fastest, most direct way. In today's time-crunched business environment, it is a big challenge just to get people to open, much less read, your e-mail message.

This part of *Writing Persuasively* will reacquaint you with writing terms and review techniques to make your writing as lean as today's typical downsized corporation.

Learn the Lingo

Grammar is a collection of terms and rules we use to discuss writing. Taught in elementary and middle school, much of this minutia about English composition may have been long forgotten by working adults.

As a general guideline, you may recall that English contains about a dozen parts of speech. Among these are *nouns*—which define persons, places, and things—and *adjectives,* which further describe those nouns. Grammarians also use various names for parts of sentences; these terms often overlap parts of speech in terminology. An example is a *subject,* which is the doer of the action. It often is a noun. Grammar terms also cover broad concepts such as *case* and *number.*

COME TO TERMS WITH THESE

Match up the grammar terms in the first column with the correct definition from the second column.

_____ 1. Adjective   A. Gives action in every sentence

_____ 2. Adverb   B. Is a person, place, or thing

_____ 3. Case   C. Receives action of a verb

_____ 4. Clause   D. Contains no subject or verb

_____ 5. Noun   E. Describes nouns and pronouns

_____ 6. Number   F. May be first, second, or third

_____ 7. Object   G. May be subjective, objective, or possessive

_____ 8. Participle   H. Often ends in "ly"

_____ 9. Person   I. Often begins with "who," "whom," "that," or "which"

_____ 10. Phrase   J. Introduces phrases

_____ 11. Preposition   K. Replaces a noun, usually for brevity

_____ 12. Pronoun   L. Connotes singular or plural

_____ 13. Verb   M. Turns a verb into an adjective

Compare your answers with the author's suggested responses in the Appendix.

Keep It Short

In persuasive writing, remember that your aim is decisive action, not prolonged negotiation. If your readers can grasp your ideas quickly, you will increase your chance of getting them to do what you want.

Use Words of Three or Fewer Syllables

Not: It is the opinion of management that employees should attempt a utilization of this innovative strategy.

But: Let's try the new plan.

Strive for an Average Sentence Length of 12 to 15 Words

Not: The New York stock market, which is used around the world as an economic indicator, has a lengthy history of downturns and recovery. To be sure, Wall Street has suffered some horrifying losses, including but not limited to the famous financial collapse that occurred in October 1929.

However, historians point out, stocks when studied in a longitudinal way prove to be one of the most optimal methods of preserving wealth.

But: The New York stock market has a history of downs and ups. The economic collapse of October 1929 is the most memorable plunge. But not the only one. Yet, despite a series of falls during the 20th century, historians say the market performs well over time.

Cut Useless Introductory Words

Not: There is a mistake on the form.

But: A mistake is on the form.

Eliminate Redundancy

Not: The manager repeated again that sales were down.

But: The manager repeated that sales were down.

Change Clauses into Adjectives

Not: The computer professional who was articulate got the promotion.

But: The articulate computer professional was promoted.

TIGHTEN AND BRIGHTEN

Review how to keep it short by circling the correct answer(s) within the following multiple-choice statements.

1. The best way to describe someone who talks a lot is (garrulous, talkative, loquacious).

2. Readers most easily comprehend sentences that are (21 words, 54 words, or 98 words) in length.

3. If your sentence contains the same meaning after eliminating these words, you should avoid beginning a statement with (subjects, pronouns, "there is").

4. (Brief moment, past experience, serious crisis) is redundant.

5. You often can improve a sentence by changing a clause into (an adjective, an adverb, a phrase).

Compare your answers with the author's suggested responses in the Appendix.

Make It Simple

If your readers get bogged down in your writing, you run the risk of losing them. But make it simple for them to read and understand—and they will be more likely to take the action you desire.

Use Mostly Simple and Compound Sentences

Not: The Best Company should strive for zero defects, which is always a solid business principle, giving customers a reason for continued loyalty.

But: The Best Company needs to strive for zero defects. This goal is a solid business principle. It also gives customers a reason for continued loyalty.

Explain Technical Data in Everyday Terms

Not: The liquid is two parts hydrogen, one part oxygen.

But: The liquid is water.

Avoid Latin-Based Abbreviations such as i.e., e.g., and etc.

Not: I am hyperventilating, i.e., I'm having difficulty breathing.

But: I'm having difficulty breathing.

Stick to Your Key Point

Not: Chicago is a great city for business. The economy is thriving there. Oprah Winfrey is a famous Chicago resident. Unemployment is less than 5%. Some of the world's largest companies maintain offices in Chicago.

But: Chicago is a great city for business. The economy is thriving there and unemployment is less than 5%. Some of the world's largest companies maintain offices in Chicago.

Use Subject/Verb/Object Sentence Structures

Not: Walking down the hall, the new vice president introduced himself.

But: The new vice president introduced himself as he was walking down the hall.

SEEK SIMPLICITY

The following statements relate to making your writing simple to read and understand. For each one, indicate whether it is true or false.

1. Complex sentences are easier to read than simple sentences.

2. Readers should be expected to look up technical terms you use in your writing.

3. Latin abbreviations are a sign of an educated writer.

4. Documents ought to stick to key points without going off onto tangents.

5. Readers can most easily understand subject-verb-object sentence structures.

Compare your answers with the author's suggested responses in the Appendix.

Write the Way You Talk

You may work for an institution but that does not mean you have to write like one. Your readers will comprehend your thoughts better if you write in a casual, conversational style.

Avoid Writing Anything You Never Say

Not: Pursuant to our conversation over the midday repast, please be advised the document requested by you is attached herewith.

But: Here's the form I mentioned at lunch.

Use Contractions as You Would in Everyday Speech

Not: I am presenting to you a pen and pencil set I would be honored for you to accept.

But: I'd like to give you this pen and pencil set.

Begin Sentences with Nouns and Pronouns

Not: Having eaten a roast beef sandwich for lunch, after which she was returning from the restaurant to the office, Sarah was struck by a car in the parking lot.

But: Sarah was hit by a car in the parking lot after lunch.

Keep Related Items Parallel

Not: The manager is good at writing, speeches, and evaluations.

But: The manager is good at writing, speaking, and giving evaluations (or evaluating).

Use Bullet Points to Break up Long Narratives

Not: When you come to computer training, please bring a notebook, a pen, your computer manual, and lots of energy.

But: For computer training, please bring your:

➤ Notebook

➤ Pen

➤ Manual

➤ Energy and enthusiasm

SAY IT CONVERSATIONALLY

Review the principles below for writing the way you talk. Each of the numbered statements that follows violates one of these standards. Put a letter by each statement to indicate which principle the statement violates. Then rewrite the example statement in a more conversational way.

A. Avoid writing anything you never say.

B. Use contractions as you would in everyday speech.

C. Begin sentences with nouns and pronouns.

D. Keep related items parallel.

E. Use bullet points to break up long narratives.

1. Per the request of facilitators, enclosed herewith are felt-tip markers.

   Problem: _____

   Improvement: _____

   _____

2. You are a wonderful speaker; I shall include this observation on the evaluation you will receive next month.

   Problem: _____

   Improvement: _____

   _____

CONTINUED

3. After eating lunch, mostly pizza, participants returned to class.

   Problem: _____

   Improvement: _____

   _____

4. The accountant asked the bookkeeper for double entries, writing neatly, and to pay more attention to details.

   Problem: _____

   Improvement: _____

   _____

5. Ryan told the job seekers to submit their resumes, fill out the forms, and call for an interview.

   Problem: _____

   Improvement: _____

   _____

Compare your answers with the author's suggested responses in the Appendix.

Get Your Readers Up to Speed

How effective will your message be if it omits essential facts or requires translation? Your readers need to match your level of understanding to get the point you are trying to make.

Include the Five Ws Early in the Document

Reason: Readers are unlikely to search through your writing to find essential points.

Not: The new company cafeteria will open soon.

But: The Impressive Company's new cafeteria will officially open at 7 A.M. Monday, Jan. 7. The gourmet eatery, open to all employees and their guests, is located on the 31st floor of corporate headquarters at 4567 Lovely St. in Chicago.

Define Terms on First Reference

Reason: Many business documents land in the hands of newcomers and outsiders unfamiliar with insider acronyms and abbreviations.

Not: FYI, the FDA will give its opinion on R2/V65 ASAP.

But: For your information, the U.S. Food and Drug Administration (FDA) says it will rule on R2/V65, The Miracle Company's new drug to help manage diabetes, as soon as possible.

Avoid Insider Jargon and Terms

Reason: Indecipherable terms are a major annoyance to your readers.

Not: IT has put out an RFP for new software documentation.

But: The Information Technology (IT) Department at The Joyful Company is seeking proposals from vendors interested in creating documentation for new software.

Spell It out When in Doubt

Reason: Many acronyms and abbreviations can be confused with others.

Not: Employees in our plant in Dublin, Ireland, should contribute to their IRAs.

But: Employees in our plant in Dublin, Ireland, should contribute to their Individual Retirement Accounts (IRA).

Identify People by Full Name, Title, and Company

Reason: You should not assume all your readers are familiar with the people mentioned in your document.

Not: Roxanne attended the meeting.

But: Roxanne Vanderbilt, vice president of marketing for The Noteworthy Company, attended the meeting.

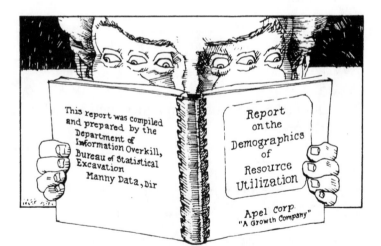

PLAY CATCH-UP WITH YOUR READERS

Review the list below of tips for getting your readers up to speed. Each of the numbered statements that follows could be improved by applying one of these suggestions. Identify the tip that should be employed by placing the appropriate letter in the space beside each statement. Then rewrite the example in a more complete way.

A.   Include the five Ws.

B.   Define terms on first reference.

C.   Check out insider jargon and terms.

D.   Spell out when in doubt.

E.   Identify people by full name, title, and company.

_____ 1. The new expense account system will go into effect. Affecting 50,000 employees on five continents, it is designed to streamline the reimbursement process.

_____

_____

_____ 2. The U.S.E.P.A. is involved in issues such as preservation of the nation's forests.

_____

_____

_____ 3. New computer users must boot up and make sure the cursor is in place before typing commands.

_____

_____

CONTINUED

CONTINUED

_____ 4. The NRA is on the third floor.

_____

_____

_____ 5. Justin will pick up the computer for the recycling program.

_____

_____

Compare your answers with the author's suggested responses in the Appendix.

Concentrate on Verbs

Verbs are the most important part of speech because they describe the action that is in a sentence. They push the sentence forward and give it momentum. Lively verbs will grab your readers' attention more readily than weaker forms.

Use Active Rather than Passive Voice

Not: The videoconferencing equipment should be used more for meetings.

But: Meeting planners should use videoconferencing more often.

Insist on Accurate Subject/Verb Agreement

Not: Each of the departments must submit their budgets for the coming year no later than Friday.

But: Each of the departments must submit its budget for the coming year no later than Friday.

Use Action Verbs

Not: The manager spoke very loudly about the need for increased sales.

But: The manager yelled about the need for increased sales.

Emphasize Straightforward, Working Verbs

Not: Tyler recommended conducting a study for examination of reports of poor customer service.

But: Tyler recommended studying reports of poor customer service.

Use Concrete Verbs

Not: Jordan seemed to be angry with Bryan about the cancelled order.

But: Jordan pounded his fist on the table and screamed at Bryan about the cancelled order.

Use Verbs with Verve

The numbered statements below are principles for using lively verbs. For each one, circle the example sentence that illustrates the principle.

1. Verb is active.

    A. The furniture was moved by the maintenance staff.

    B. The maintenance staff moved the furniture.

2. Verb agrees with its subject.

    A. Neither Sally nor Greta are going out for lunch.

    B. Neither Sally nor Greta is going out for lunch.

3. Verb connotes action.

    A. The injured bookkeeper moved really slowly on crutches across the floor

    B. The injured bookkeeper limped on crutches across the floor.

4. Verb is straightforward.

    A. The manager made a decision to cut the budget.

    B. The manager decided to cut the budget.

5. Verb is concrete.

    A. The assistant appeared distraught when he read the news.

    B. The assistant slammed the report on the desk and stomped out when he read news.

Compare your answers with the author's suggested responses in the Appendix.

Accentuate the Positive

Negative language and dictates repel many readers, which is not the response you want when you are trying to persuade them to your way of thinking. Instead, you can help create a positive reaction with the words you choose.

Eliminate Not When Possible

Not: The proposal won't be ready until Monday.

But: The proposal will be ready Monday.

Emphasize Rewards, Not Punishments

Not: If you don't come to work on time, you'll be fired.

But: If you come to work on time, you'll keep your job.

Not: If our company does not purchase a new trade-show display, our customers will think our business is hurting.

But: If we purchase a new trade-show display, our customers will think we're in tune with the latest trends.

Be Wary of Loaded Words

Not: We're unable to find the check you claim you sent us.

But: We're unable to find the check you said you sent Sept. 26.

Avoid Commands

Not: Our company should participate in this charity car wash.

But: Participating in this charity car wash will be a way to give back to the community.

Soften Imperative Sentences and Drop False Urgency

Not: Go. Do it. Now.

But: Please complete the task before noon.

Not: Change it today or forget it for this year.

But: If you will make this change today, we'll be set for the rest of the year.

SAY YES TO YOUR READERS

The memo below exemplifies how *not* to write persuasively. Rewrite the memo in a positive, motivational manner, using the following techniques discussed in this section:

➤ Keep it short

➤ Make it simple

➤ Write the way you talk

➤ Get your readers up to speed

➤ Concentrate on verbs

➤ Accentuate the positive

Sample Memo

To: The Sloppy Company Employees
From: Jake Neatnick, CEO
Date: March 28
Re: Clean up your act!

Once again, I am not pleased with the response, or lack thereof, to my pleas for a cleanup of our manufacturing plant. As Sloppy employees, you must get your act together once and for all and rid the facility of your filthy trash. I'm well aware that several of you claim to have spent last weekend dumping crap, but I see little evidence of this contention. If you don't clean up by the first of next month, I am going to deduct enough money from your paycheck to bring in a professional cleaning crew. So stop putting this off. Get to work. And I mean immediately.

Compare your answers with the author's suggested responses in the Appendix.

Relax Grammar Rules as Appropriate

When you are writing to sell, your readers want and need to get your message quickly. In the interest of getting to the point, you can sometimes bend a few grammar rules to punch up your writing and move readers along. The key is *appropriateness* to the context.

Use First and Second Person

Not: The Caring Company is excited about the sales increase.

But: We're excited about our company's sales increase. We hope you are, too.

End Sentences with Prepositions

Not: This is the kind of baseless complaint with which I can't deal.

But: This is the kind of baseless complaint I can't deal with.

Split Infinitives as Needed

Not: The manager seems to want this new policy a lot.

But: The manager seems to really want this new policy.

Avoid Making a Federal Case out of Case

Not: It is I on the telephone.

But: It's me on the line.

Allow Sentence Fragments

Not: You have a great idea. I'll meet you for lunch at noon.

But: Great! See you at noon.

TAKE A BREAK

The following sentences are from e-mails to employees of a small company. They all break traditional grammar rules. Answer whether you would change them or let them stand, as is, for informal writing.

_____ A. The Pleasant Company wants to brag! We've signed our first $1 million contract.

_____ B. I don't understand what Stan called the meeting for.

_____ C. The accountant was urged to quietly watch the suspected embezzler.

_____ D. The culprit is me.

_____ E. Done deal! Hooray!

Compare your answers with the author's suggested responses in the Appendix.

Part 5 Summary

Put a check (✔) in the box next to ideas that you intend to use in your next writing project:

❏   Transmit information in the most direct way.

❏   State everything as succinctly as possible.

❏   Express your thoughts clearly and simply.

❏   Cut words and phrases you never say in spoken language.

❏   Fill your readers in on the background of your topic.

❏   Improve verbs in a variety of ways.

❏   Keep your reader on your side with positive affirmation.

❏   Relax grammar rules that detract from punchy persuasive writing.

APPENDIX

Author's Suggested Responses

Part 1: Rethink Sales

Identify the Writer's Goal (Page 5)

Possible responses include:

2. Contribute money.

3. Prevent executives from getting upset.

4. Believe the Hawaii expense was well spent.

5. Approve increase in manpower.

6. Get a large turnout at the meeting

7. Persuade the temporary to take the permanent job.

Case Study: Compare These Salespeople (Page 7)

The correct response is Emily. She has a better future in sales than Amanda because she spends only a few minutes building rapport before getting to the point of her sales call.

Analyze Your Own Reading Behavior (Pages 9-10)

The answer most likely to be given by today's busy readers to all 10 questions is "never."

Part 2: Use the S.A.L.E.S. Model

Recognize the S.A.L.E.S. Technique (Page 19)

1. Salespeople got customers' attention by asking a question: "Which team are you rooting for?"

2. Essentials and features were answered by the five Ws:

   ➤ What channels the TV gets

   ➤ Who makes it

   ➤ When it can be shipped

   ➤ Where to get service

   ➤ Why you should own it

3. Benefits:

   ➤ TV is on sale

   ➤ It is the latest technology

   ➤ You need to keep up with the Joneses

4. Countering objections:

   ➤ Refrigerators are on sale too

   ➤ Orthodontist can be paid over time

   ➤ If you lose your job, you can enjoy this TV

5. Sign-off: Salespeople offer a choice of finishes, delivery, and payment options.

The S.A.L.E.S. Model in Writing (Page 20)

The first word of each sentence starts each part of the S.A.L.E.S. model.

   You...   (S)
   Thanks...(A)
   Bridget... (L)
   I...   (E)
   If...   (S)

Choose the More Persuasive Sentence (Pages 21-22)

The correct responses are: 1) B; 2) A; 3) B; 4) B; 5) A.

Hook Your Reader (Page 24)

Below is a possible opening statement you might use in the scenario involving recruitment of the cross-functional team to prepare a report on rewarding employees who provide excellent customer service:

Interested in traveling around the world while making a valuable contribution to The Cash Company? Read on!

Describe the Big Picture (Page 27)

Below is a possible background paragraph you might use in the scenario involving recruitment of the cross-functional team to prepare a report on rewarding employees who provide excellent customer service:

Nigel Whitethorn, vice president of Human Resources, has asked me to recruit 12 people to serve for six months on a cross-functional committee to study ways of rewarding outstanding customer service by our employees. And we want you! The group will start work the first of next month in London. We then will meet in Los Angeles, Beijing, Bangalore, and Rome before making our final recommendations in London.

Tell Readers What's in It for Them (Page 30)

Below is a possible benefits paragraph you might use in the scenario involving recruitment of the cross-functional team to prepare a report on rewarding employees who provide excellent customer service:

Obviously, serving on this committee will give you the opportunity to visit several continents to solidify relationships with other members. Taking on this job also will give you the opportunity to:

➤ *Network face to face with executives and staff in our international offices.*

➤ *Increase your understanding of the global marketplace.*

➤ *Learn about cross-cultural issues affecting all businesses.*

➤ *Influence the implementation of the new rewards policy.*

➤ *Earn the gratitude of Nigel Whitethorn and The Cash Company.*

Answer Objections Before They Come Up (Page 33)

Below is a possible counter paragraph you might use in the scenario involving recruitment of the cross-functional team to prepare a report on rewarding employees who provide excellent customer service:

All that being said about benefits, I realize that Nigel and I are asking for a huge time commitment on your part. And, like all of us at The Cash Company, you undoubtedly have plenty of work to keep you busy. Knowing this, Nigel has authorized me to tell you that he plans to provide all committee members with new, state-of-the-art, time-saving organization and e-mail equipment while you're on the road. It will be yours to keep, of course, after this assignment is over.

Ask Readers to Take Action (Page 35)

Below is a possible sign-off you might use in the scenario involving recruitment of the cross-functional team to prepare a report on rewarding employees who provide excellent customer service:

Because Nigel regards the new rewards system as priority one during the next two quarters, he would like an immediate response. You can reach me by replying to this e-mail, sending an interoffice memo, or calling me at 555-4444.

Dissect This Document (Pages 36-37)

For several decades...   (S)
This proposal is for...   (A)
The benefits for...   (L)
Yes, although...   (E)
We at Overlooked...   (S)

Sell Your Own Idea (Page 38)

Here's a sample of the kind of document you might write on the job:

```
To: Erin O'Connor
From: Xian Lee
Date: Feb. 3, 2002
Re: You Should Order Bulk Copies of This Writing Book

Erin,

When you gave me a copy of Writing Persuasively to
read, I must admit I felt a bit defensive. As a com-
puter programmer with English as a second language, I
am sensitive about my business communications skills.
Having read the book and done the exercises, I have
to say that I learned a lot. In fact, I think we
should order copies for all 500 people in Information
Technology at our company.

I believe strongly that Writing Persuasively would
help all our techies get away from computer-speak
into plain English. Arranged in five easy-to-read
sections, the book focuses specifically on ways non-
salespeople can use classic sales techniques to get
across their ideas. Written by Kathleen A. Begley, a
professional writer and trainer, the book can be
purchased over the web at www.crisplearning.com.

The books would be of great benefit to our entire
team, most of whom spent all their school years
studying math and science rather than writing and
other communication. Specifically, Writing Persua-
sively would enable us to:
```

- Sell our proposals more effectively.

- Influence budget decisions to our advantage.

- Learn how to translate complex information for the
  general audience.

- Become more confident when writing to non-computer people.

- Explain our ideas and products to the marketing department.

To be sure, any expenditure is difficult in these uncertain economic times. But I think the price of continued bad writing is even worse. For a fraction of what it would cost us to put people through live classroom training, we can provide copies of <u>Writing Persuasively</u> to everyone involved in technology.

Once you authorize the money, I'll be happy to order the books and distribute them to all our people. Do you think we should order 500 or 550 copies?

Xian

Part 3: Involve Your Readers' Senses

Make It Visual, Tactile, or Auditory (Page 48)

Many responses are correct. The key is to write differently to people based on their visual, tactile, and auditory preferences. In the scenario involving The Dangerous Company's interest in increasing attendance at monthly safety meetings, here are some ways you might do this:

Visual

Words: Use words such as "see," "look," "view," "image," and "picture."

Sentences: Appeal to sight with sentences such as "Picture this: If we all faithfully attend safety meetings, there will be no ugly accident scenes in the news media."

Graphics: Include pie charts and bar graphs showing the relationship of attendance at safety meetings to a decrease in industrial accidents.

Enclosures: Send a colorful t-shirt with a slogan regarding the safety meetings.

Packaging: Enclose the information in a professionally designed presentation folder.

Tactile

Words: Use words such as "touch," "feel," "soft," "cold," and "wet."

Sentences: Appeal to touch with sentences such as "At The Dangerous Company, many safety signs say 'Do Not Touch.' But these written warnings are not enough to ensure an accident-free workplace."

Graphics: Include pie charts and bar graphs involving tactile features of explosions such as heat.

Enclosures: Send a rubber stress-reducing ball imprinted with a safety slogan.

Packaging: Enclose the information in a textured presentation folder.

Auditory

Words: Use words such as "hear," "noise," "loud," "thundering," and "crash."

Sentences: Appeal to hearing with sentences such as "Kaboom! The sound of an explosion is something we never want to hear within one of the plants at The Dangerous Company."

Graphics: Include set-off quotes from people talking about the noise and chaos of industrial explosions.

Enclosures: Send a mug with a safety-related scene involving peace and quiet.

Packaging: Enclose the information in a quiet-looking blue or green folder.

Translate This Document (Pages 54-55)

Driver Style

May 8
Michael Lee
The High Tech Company
123 Silicon Blvd.
Palo Alto, CA

Dear Mr. Lee,

Thanks for writing. We appreciate your bringing to our attention the problem you encountered recently with one of our customer service representatives. We regret any inconvenience this situation has caused you.

After receiving your letter stating that one of our employees had used profane language toward you as you were placing an order during a telephone conversation in April, we thoroughly investigated the matter. Based on interviews and evidence, we've decided to let the employee go for his unacceptable behavior. You are a valued customer and we are committed to making a strong response to your complaint.

But we want to go a step farther. In an effort to create a good relationship with your firm, we'd like to offer you three months free service on the telecommunications networking you expressed interest in. We care about your bottom line just as we care about our own.

If you'd like further discussion, call me any time during business hours at the number listed on this stationery.

Sincerely,
Olga

Part 4: Adapt Additional Sales Techniques

Put It All Together (Page 71)

Your S.A.L.E.S. proposal should follow the five-paragraph model. It needs to emphasize career and financial benefits to Renee for taking the course in a live, classroom setting.

```
To: Renee Gifford
From: Your Coach
Date: June 4
Re: A live class will save you time!
```

Time—it certainly is the most precious commodity of the 21st century. Renee, I appreciate your desire to take training courses in the most efficient way. As you said during our phone conversation, you are an extremely busy manager here at The Major Company.

To be frank, however, I must re-emphasize that the latest research shows that live, in-classroom training produces better and faster results than online learning in certain topics. And one of those topics is managerial communication skills. According to research done by leading training organizations, participants master skills such as giving feedback and motivating staff best by practicing role plays and discussing case studies with their peers. I recommend strongly that you enroll in "People Skills: The Key to Career Success" being offered during the first five work days of every month this year at our off-site company training center in Boston.

From a learning viewpoint, you'll receive many benefits from the live training. Specifically, you'll be able to:

- Master communications skills faster and easier in the long-run.

- Learn from observing others in a classroom setting.

- Receive valuable real-time feedback from your instructor.

- Practice techniques in front of your colleagues.

- Focus on the topic without at-home distractions.

To be sure, in this electronic age, classroom learning seems like a dinosaur. And it may be—in certain topics, particularly those involving rote learning such as setting up computers or balancing ledgers. But not for topics involving people skills.

Because of your busy schedule, I have already checked availability at the next classes. There is still space at the next three scheduled workshops. Would you like to sign up for the class in July, August, or September?

Part 5: Get to the Point

Come to Terms with These (Page 76)

The correct responses are 1. E; 2. H; 3. G; 4. I; 5. B; 6. L; 7. C; 8. M; 9. F; 10. D; 11. J; 12. K; 13. A.

Tighten and Brighten (Page 78)

The correct responses are 1. talkative; 2. 21 words; 3. there is; 4. all; 5. adjective.

Seek Simplicity (Page 80)

The correct responses are 1. false; 2. false; 3. false; 4. true; 5. true.

Say It Conversationally (Pages 82-83)

The principles are:

1. **Problem:**   Writing the way you talk

   Improvement: Here are the felt-tip markers the teachers asked me to send you.

2. **Problem:**   Using contractions

   Improvement: You're a wonderful speaker; I'll include this observation on the evaluation you'll receive next month.

3. **Problem:**   Beginning with nouns and pronouns

   Improvement: Participants returned to class after eating pizza for lunch.

4. **Problem:**   Keeping related items parallel

   Improvement: The accountant asked the bookkeeper to make double entries, write neatly, and pay more attention to details.

5. **Problem:**   Using bullet points instead of classic transitions

   Improvement: Ryan told the jobseekers they needed to:

   - Submit their resumes
   - Fill out the forms
   - Call for an interview

Play Catch-up with Your Readers (Pages 86-87)

The missing items are:

1. A

The Nice Company's new expense system will go into effect July 1, 2002, affecting all our 50,000 employees on five continents. It's designed to streamline the reimbursement process.

2. B or D

The U.S. Environmental Protection Agency (EPA) is involved in issues such as preservation of the nation's forests.

3. C

New computer users should read the manual or get personal instruction about steps necessary to use word-processing software.

4. D

The Nathan Reagan Agency is on the third floor.

5. E

Justin Murphy, administrative assistant in the marketing department at The Dollar Company, will pick up the Dell 386 computer from Room 876 at company headquarters. He will donate it to the Westtown recycling program.

Use Verbs with Verve (Page 89)

The correct responses are 1. B; 2. B; 3. A; 4. B; 5. B.

Say Yes to Your Readers (Page 91)

There is no one correct revision. The point is to eliminate negative expressions. Here's an example of a more positive document:

```
To: The Sloppy Company Employees
From: Jake Neatnick, CEO
Date: March 28
Re: I need your help!

Clean is keen! And we will be conducting a major
cleanup of our manufacturing plant next week. I need
everyone to pitch in on this three-day campaign so
that we avoid getting cited for poor housekeeping
during government or customer inspections. Believe
me, I know you're all busy and have more interesting
things to do than sweep the floor and throw out
trash—but this cleanup is critical to our long-term
success. Please respond by specifying which day next
week you can devote to the campaign—Monday,Tuesday,
or Wednesday.
```

Take a Break (Page 93)

All five samples are acceptable in informal e-mail to people you know well but not to outsiders you have never met.

Be forewarned, however, that strict grammarians within your organization may argue with your use of second person, an ending preposition, a split infinitive, objective case, and a sentence fragment as shown in the five examples. So be sure you can explain the rule you're breaking—and why! Ideally, your deviation from tradition should make your writing easier to understand for today's busy reader.

Recommended Reading

Andrus, Carol. *Fat-Free Writing*. Boston, MA: Thomson Learning/Course Technology, 2001.

Bozek, Phillip. *50 One-Minute Steps to Better Communication*. Boston, MA: Thomson Learning/Course Technology, 1997.

Bly, Robert. *Selling Your Services*. New York: Henry Holt, 1991.

Brock, Susan. *Better Business Writing*. Boston, MA: Thomson Learning/Course Technology, 1997.

Ferrara, Cosmo. *Writing on the Job*. New York: Prentice-Hall, 1995.

Fitzgerald, Suzanne Sparks. *Great Business Writing*. New York: McGraw-Hill, 1999.

Joseph, Albert. *Put It In Writing*. New York: McGraw-Hill, 1998.

Kennedy, Dan S. *The Ultimate Sales Letter*. Holbrook, MA: Adams Media, 2000.

Lesonsky, Rieva. *Start Your Own Business*. Irvine, CA: Entrepreneur Press, 2001.

Lewis, Herschell Gordon. *Sales Letters That Sizzle*. Chicago: NTC Books, 1999.

Manning, Marilyn. *Professionalism in the Office*. Boston, MA: Thomson Learning/Course Technology, 2001.

Piotrowski, Maryann V. *Effective Business Writing*. New York: HarperCollins, 1996.

Roman, Kenneth and Raphaelson, Joel. *Writing That Works*. New York: HarperCollins, 2000.

Rosenweig, David. *Spend Less, Sell More*. Chicago: Probus, 1995.

Ross, Marilyn. *Shameless Marketing for Brazen Hussies*. Buena Vista, CO: Communication Creativity, 2000.

Tronnes, Mike. *Closers: Great American Writers on the Art of Selling*. New York: St. Martin's Press, 1998.

Wienbroer, Diana Roberts, Hughes, Elaine, and Silverman, Jay. *Rules of Thumb for Business Writers*. New York: McGraw-Hill, 2000.